The Colour of Love

The Colour of Love

Poems from the Heart

STEPHEN CASSETTARI

CALLIGRAPHY BY

ANGELA CASSETTARI

Angus&Robertson
An imprint of HarperCollins*Publishers*

For Angela —
wife, mother, companion, lover,
artist and special friend.

An Angus & Robertson Publication

Angus&Robertson, an imprint of
HarperCollins*Publishers*
25 Ryde Road, Pymble, Sydney, NSW 2073, Australia
31 View Road, Glenfield, Auckland 10, New Zealand

First published in Australia in 1994 19/7/95

National Library of Australia
Cataloguing-in-Publication data:

Cassettari, Stephen.
The colour of love.
ISBN 0 207 18209 4.
1. Love poetry, Australian. I. Title.
A821.3

Printed in Hong Kong

9 8 7 6 5 4 3 2 1
98 97 96 95 94

Foreword

Many people do not openly express their love for one another. Instead they hesitate to show their true selves and hide behind 'masks'. They hold their hands at their sides when they should be embracing their loved ones and making the most of every precious moment of their lives. I often think: if only people could come to terms with their uncertainty and really show their feelings, they would be more peaceful with themselves.

I hope that the following poems, paintings and calligraphy will give people the inspiration to be more expressive with their thoughts and feelings.

Carl Cassettari

June 1993

Introduction

My parents, through the daily expression of their love for one another over 45 years, have been a shining example to my wife Angela and myself. They've taught us that love is the greatest of all gifts.

The love that we have for each other is expressed in this book through the arts of the Oriental brush. In the traditional manner, poetry, calligraphy and painting are connected here and are manifestations of the head, hand and heart.

The poems bring out the essence of the spirit in all of us. The paintings, sensual in their colour, form and subject, further enhance the content of the poems and transcend the limits of words. The visual impact of the gracious calligraphy also enhances the meaning of the words. Thus, the three forms of expression join together to breathe the spirit of love.

I believe when one heart merges with another, the separateness that divides the world is reduced and the greater being of 'oneness' is closer to realization. The contents of this book can be applied to any situation where one heart meets with another, whether it is two strangers, a brother and sister or two lovers. I hope that many hearts are joined through this book.

Flower of love
in the centre
of my garden.
This is
but a small tear
of joy
in the ocean
of our love.

The colour of love
fills my eyes
with golden tears
and warms my heart
with JOY
through the melting
silver years.

Love is a mirror.
The longer you look
the more
there is to see.
You are the lake
where the moon dwells
on earth.
The poet
walks upon the shore –
a quiet companion
under the
silent song
of the stars.

A gentle touch
will open a
HEART
where the strength
of many words
will fail.

Let not love
hold too tight
the gossamer wings of
DESIRE.
But rather
let love
lightly caress
the tender heart.

You hold my hand
and waves of warmth
fill the silence.
You gaze into my eyes
and I drown
in the ocean
of your love.

Each day unfolds
a new petal
around the flower of
LOVE.
Singing in glorious
colours
to a soft
shimmering world.

Watching moments
of your movements
my eyes caress
every curve.
In your stillness
of slumber
your love
warms the room.

Today
from a distance
my love
TOUCHES
you.
Enfolded
in memories
with the mists
of yesterday.

Dear heart
that beats with mine.
Our togetherness
reflects the heart
that lives in everyone.
Through our union
all the world
draws closer
and holds us
in its embrace.

Within our
daughter's eyes
your face gazes out.
Her young body moves
in shadow echoes
of your

BEING.

Yesterday
becomes today
in growing love.

First child
growing within,
love glowing without.
Roundness,
completeness,
the wonder of you.

Our children
are treasures
from the deep
sea of love.
Our art is our song
from creation above.

Baby at your breast,
hope in your heart.
No words to express
endless tenderness.

Children
are the living proof
of the glory of love.

To see a glimpse of you
in the distance
among a crowd.
Our eyes meet
for a moment
and you are as
CLOSE
as the inside
of my heart.

In all the wanderings
of our love,
the moon has been our
constant companion.
Her face in the night
CALMS
the waters
of our sorrow
and mellows the
shadows of our passion.

The morning mist
creeps through the
open window,
enshrouding us in
its cool
EMBRACE.
The warm summer night
has left us
fresh with desire.

After a night of love,
rain drips
from the trees
as if
the world has melted
in the passion
of our embrace.

Within the mist
and shadows
rivers run
through the forest.
Climbing
the mountain of desire
to float
amid the clouds.

Distance
does not separate us.
You surround me
like another
BODY.
Your presence
moves within me
when I feel
the touch
of your hand.

You display your heart
with soft words
of kindness.
Your eyes
GLOW
with the fires within.
In the quiet surrender
of a tender moment,
words are as distant
as yesterday.

Walk with me
on this fair night,
that we may travel
some distance together.
Your tread is
LIGHT
upon the earth,
your laughter
lifts to the stars.

Melting moments
in lingering love,
caressing embrace
for honest heart.

Together touching
in kindness kiss,
gentle glowing
your calming quiet.

The tears of my love
flow from the depths
of my heart
and are changed
by the
FIRE
of your love
into crystals of joy
that reflect
the beauty of you.

Be gentle with
my wounded
SOUL
lest the blood
dripping from my eyes
may stain your
tender heart.

Captured
by your charms again,
let us fall in love again.
Don't break my heart,
don't let us part.
HOLD
me in your arms again,
this time
it will never end.

The dance enfolds
the moment—
eyes embrace
the heart's expanse.

Love never dies.
Love only changes.
Expanding
we embrace
the changes
in each other.

The arms of my love
will always hold you
in soft embrace.
The warmth
of my love
will always
SHINE
on your loving face.

What

WONDER

of rhymeless reason
this mystery of love.
Expressed in one
reflected in many.

You depart –
your memory lingers
through the day.
You return –
your presence
fills the memory.

Two hearts
together
to touch.
TRUE
love
is never
too much.

One moment,
one forever,
one love,
one together.